This Journal Belongs To

_____

That's what people who love do, they put their arms around you and love you when you're not so loveable

– Deb Caeltti

Love is patient and kind; Love doesnot envy or boast; it is not ar
rogant or rude. It does not insist on it's own way; it is not irritable
or resentful; it does note rejoice at wrongdoing, but rejoices with
truth - 1 Corinthians 13:4-6

Less is more...

except when it comes to love, and then more is more is more

Enjoy the little things, for one day you may look back and re
alise they were the big things.
- Robert Brault

All you need is love. But a little chocolate now and then doesn't hurt. - Charlze M. Shuulz

My body needs laughter as much as it eeds tears. Both are cleansers of stress. - Mahogany SilverRain

As soon as you're trying to please everyone else you actually have time to make yourself happy. - Delaney Curry

It's never too late to be who you might have been.
- George Eliot

The groundwork of all happiness is health.
    - James Leigh Hunt

Sometimes nothing is the best thing to say and often the best thing to do - Michael Thomas Sunnarborg

What can you do to promote world peace? Go home and love your family - Mother Teresa

We spend precious hours fearing the inevitable. It would be wise to use that time adoring our families, cherishing our friends and living our lives. - Maya Angelou

All truly great thoughts are conceived while walking.
- Friedrich Nietzsche

No act of kindness, however small . Is never wasted - Aesop

A good laugh is sunshine in the house. - William Thackeray

It is not how much we have, but how much we enjoy that makes happiness. - Charels Spurgeon

Together in our house, in the firelight, we are the world made small. - Jennifer Donnelly

If you judge people, you have no time to love them.
Mother Teresa

Your relationship with others are always a direct reflection of the relationship you have with yourself.

- Michael Thomas Sunnarborg

Happiness resides not in possessions, and not in gold, happiness dwells in the soul. - Democtitus

The love between a mother and their child will be forever tied
- Melissa Desveaux

Everyone must leave something behind when they die. Your legacy is every life you touch. - Maya Angelou

I would rather my heart be without words than my words be without heart. - LaMar Boschman

You've gotta dance like there's nobody watching, Love like you'll never be hurt, Sing like there's nobody listening, And live like it's heaven on earth. – William W. Purkey

You never lose by loving . You always lose by holding back .
– Barbara De Angelis

Being deeply loved by someone gives you strength, while loving someone deeply gives you courage. – Lao Tzu

Love is more than a noun — it is a verb; it is more than a feeling — it is caring , sharing , helping , sacrificing .
— William Arthur Ward

Love is a choice you make from moment to moment.
— Barbara De Angelis

Love is an ocean of emotions entirely surrounded by expenses. –
Thomas Dewar

Better to have loved and lost, than to have never loved at all.
– St. Augustine

Where there is love there is life. – Mahatma Gandhi

A loving heart is the truest wisdom. – Charles Dickens

To be brave is to love someone unconditionally, without expecting anything in return. – Madonna

The chance to love and be loved exists no matter where you are. – Oprah Winfrey

I believe there are some things in life you can't deny or rationalize, and [love] is one of them. – Cate Blanchett

You know it's love when all you want is that person to be happy, even if you're not part of their happiness.
– Julia Roberts

A new command I give you: Love one another. As I have loved you, so you must love one another. – Jesus Christ

No one has ever seen God; if we love one another, God abides in us and his love is perfected in us.- 1 John 4:12

Above all, keep loving one another earnestly, since love covers a multitude of sins. - 1 Peter 4:8

We love because he first loved us. - 1 John 4:19

For God gave us a spirit not of fear but of power and love and self -control. - 2 Timothy 1:7

Greater love has no one than this, that someone lay down his life for his friends. - John 15:13

But I say to you, love your enemies and pray for those who persecute you. - Matthew 5:44

Love does no wrong to a neighbor; therefore love is the fulfilling of the law. - Romans 13:10

There is no fear in love, but perfect love casts out fear. For fear has to do with punishment, and whoever fears has not been perfected in love. - 1 John 4:18

Love makes you appreciate things about a person that you might not normally like.

Love takes a lot of work to get through the hard times.

Great loves don't always last forever, so love like there's no tomorrow.

You don't have to be the smartest person in the world to know what love is.

Love can be the most random person, in the most random place: embrace it.

When you love, you love through the good and the bad times.

Love is as much an intellectual attraction as it is a physical one.

We accept the love we think we deserve. – Charlie, The Perks of Being a Wallflower

A person needs to be able to love themselves in order to feel love for someone else.

I was hiding under your porch because I love you. –Dug, UP

Because when I look at you, I can feel it. And I look at you and I'm home." – Dory, Finding Nemo

Some people are worth melting for. – Olaf, Frozen

You are my greatest adventure.
– Mr. Incredible, The Incredibles

Listen with your heart. You will understand.
– Grandmother Willow, Pocahontas

Ohana means family. Family means nobody gets left behind .
—Lilo and Stitch, Lilo & Stitch

Everything is different now that I see you.
– Flynn Rider and Rapunzel, Tangled

No matter how your heart is grieving, if you keep on believing, the dream that you wish will come true.
– Cinderella, Cinderella

A true hero isn't measured by the size of his strength, but by the strength of his heart. - Hercules, 'Hercules'.

How do you spell love? You don't spell love. You feel it.

- Piglet and Pooh, 'Winnie The Pooh'

Life may be swift and fleeting . Hope may die yet love's
beautiful music. Comes each day like the dawn.
- Bambi

Today's special moments are tomorrow's memories.
- Aladdin